February! 2022

ON EARTH

AND

IN

Dearest Mack,

I think of you a lot with so much love.

Here's hoping you can find a poem you like in this whole bunch.

Gretchen

also by Gretchen Lara-Shartle

Awakening Courage

Dare to Adventure, Las Bienaventuranzas:
The Life of Jorge Lara-Braud

ON EARTH
AND
IN HEAVEN

poems by Gretchen Lara-Shartle

paintings by Irma Grizá

Good Adventure Press
Austin, Texas

With love for my daughters
Greta and Kyria

Contents

My Joy

For me, poetry is finding images and allowing them to
speak.
Images surprise me before Eucharist in church,
while planting or walking.
One midnight in a Taos, New Mexico park
the fun of playing on swings
and slides kindled thoughts,
and the experience gave rise to poems.
It's a serendipity
when images without
and feelings within
begin to know each other.
The real work is effecting that union,
then giving it a voice which may touch another.
Inspiration is a grace;
giving it expression is my choice.

Gretchen Lara-Shartle

On Earth and In Heaven

There is the up and downness of the slide,
    the back and forthness of the swing,
    or simply standing on earth
    and looking at the stars.

The slide's not bad for play,
    but watch the jolt.
Swinging's fun.
The earth moves everywhere
    with you.
Then, you come back to the same place.

Being on the ground
    watching heaven is good too.

Tree by the Waters

Yes Lord! the tree—standing alone
    by the flowing stream,
    steady, upward reaching trunk.

Yes, I will stand firm,
    my spine—its trunk.

Allow me to be deeply rooted,
    to reach down into earthen serenity
    like the roots of the tree,
    the one by the waters.

Boosts of Loveliness

All around my house I find them—
    boosts of loveliness.
I put them there.

Sometimes, as I look at them, I wonder:
    "Will you be in my dreams tonight?"
Outside my window,
    a spiral shell
    sheltered by falling green leaves,
    comes together in one single point.
On my shoulders is a shawl of rose
    woven through lavender and gray.
Before me is the black cross
    standing in blue,
    symbol of communication,
    reminder that pain
    sometimes leads to greater life.

My metate* altar
    alive with burning candles,
    the stone where women before
    ground corns into meal,
    the place where I knead loneliness
    into fullness.

* Metate is a stone used for grinding corn.

Forging Ṛta

I remember the Brahmin priest
    gathering white, starred flowers
    in the Bengali village
    near Shantiniketan—place of peace.
Bringing Ṛta into this world
    takes priests, workers, flowers.

When do we need to stand firm
    holding our knives,
    or simply move with the flow?
First, to balance tenderly
    like the lady crossing the wire,
    holding her rod as she moves,
    listening to innards
    without losing sight of the field.
Then, armed with the star of faith,
    take jumps to yes or no.

When forging Ṛta,
    it helps to remember the old Brahmin
    gathering flowers
    for a holy ritual alone.
That grounding makes it easier
    to know when to stand firm,
    or simply to laugh and be
    while building the place of peace.

(Ṛta is a Sanskirt word for order in the microcosm and macrocosm.)

Tree of Grace

Down there in the bare hull alone,
        how could I sing?
The blonde child of my dreams was dying.
Finally, alone, I sowed.
Later, a trace of green showed.

I wept for the little one
        then let him go
        together with hopes to grow love
        in a garden tended by too few.

Strengthened by looking,
        I gathered that touch of green
        and listened beneath the silence.

Then, I saw the tree of grace
        in the sun with bells.

Japanese Stones

She walks the Japanese stoned path,
    her heart unafraid, body bare,
    even her arms see.
As she lifts one foot,
    her right foot anchored warm,
    grips the smooth stone beneath.

In that moment,
    simply feeling the love
    of twilight bathing
    not trying, just knowing.

Picking Up Stones

Step by step . . .
    she picked up stones,
    then put them in her wagon.

As a child moving freely,
    now too, I like pulling stones
    from the earth, laying them aside.

Sometimes, I lose sight
    of that child
    moving along
    picking up stones
    and putting them in her wagon.

Those are the days
    when I can't let them go,
    and they get heavy.

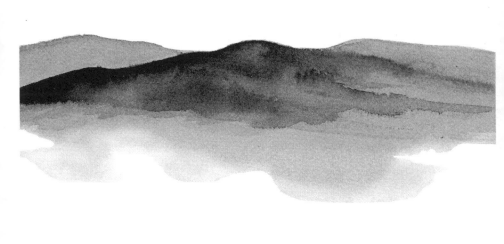

Strengthening

Look to the hills for strength.
Sit with your back straight.
Know the warmth of your own shawl.

My darlin', wait awhile
    for your heart to quieten.
When you see your fears
    let them go.
Clear waters can be your teacher.
Emulate their clarity.

Loving and being loved
    is a deep part of strengthening,
    but can we make that happen?

Making a New Path

As I search, I move
    and make a new path.

I look for a way
    not marked by ancient ones,
    a path to make my own,
    where another
    will sometimes walk with me.

Often, I will be there
    knowing my heart
    in the deepest aloneness.

Silent Strength

I seek straight tree trunks
   standing like posts of silent strength
   in darkening space at twilight.

Lights Touching
in Wild Cat Hollow

She, alone, waiting in patience,
    not jumping at the first thing,
    went walking in Wild Cat Hollow.

Walking, listening, constant crickets—
    Texas sounds had comforted her years.

Watching puffed gray-apricot clouds,
    she fills her insides.

Descending Harbor View,
    she sees
    lights in communion,
    barely touching.

Pulling in Her Nets

Her body jagged,
    she'd promised herself by Easter
    her insides would be lightened.

Now September.
Spotlights shine on the sickly man
    from her dreams.
His body bloodless, he whispers,
    "You may lose your beloved,"
    and pulls her to him.
Her friend presses:
    "Never let him stop you!
    Let go and be joyful!"

Then, by turning her focus,
    her body smooths.
Like those Galilean fishermen,
    she tugs, pulls in her nets
    and catches that instant.
While holding the nets close,
    she lets go his fearful whisperings
    and keeps the fish with shining eyes.

She feels her veins open,
    her blood move
    and simply enjoys her own rhythms.

a new embrace

yesterday
    on the phone
        i said i want you to hold me

your words
    rose feathered wings
        held me

swinging lettuce dry

washed green lettuce
    in netted wire
i swing it round and round,
      circling the house
         sprinkling plants
           with droplets

i like loving moving swinging
being still in green circles
    is a blessing too

A Reaching Prayer

Strengthen me
    to give lovingly
        from deeper centers,
    to let go fears
        of my dark side.

Under the wide reaching oak boughs,
    are light and shadows.

Like the oak,
    I too can embrace frailties,
    enter shadows
        and learn from them.

Let my backbone rise
    like the oak's trunk.

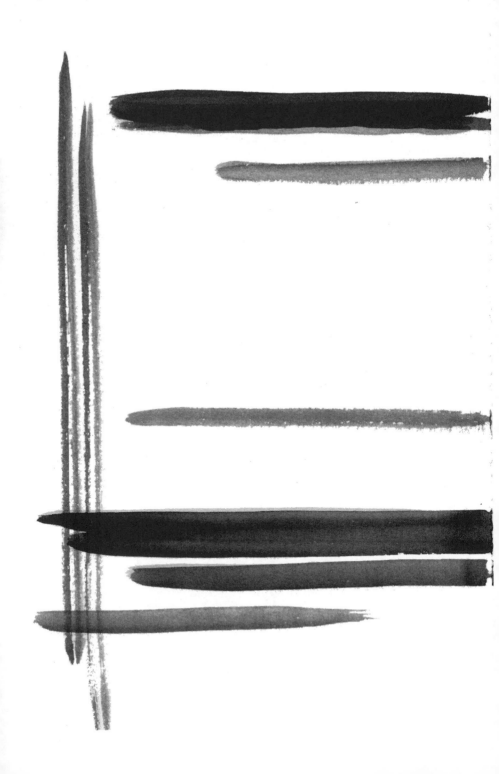

Lines and Edges

"Que Dios te bendiga . . ."*

The half-moon held glowing beauty
    in her cupped hands
    this Christmas Eve at midnight.

The hilltop rim of the chapel patio
    paralleled horizon's edge.

Together, they smoothed my forehead lines
    as Mother's long fingers once did.

*"Que Dios te bendiga" means "may God bless you."

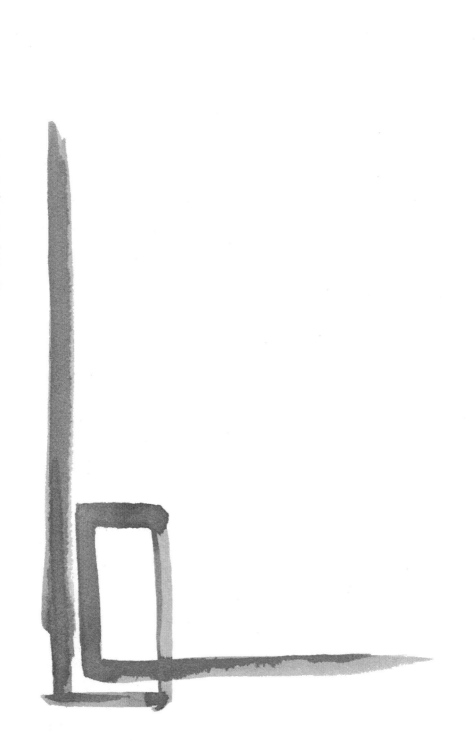

Tending Boundaries

I felt deeply alone without her
    and feared the impending loss of him.

His words, like that hot August sun,
    kept pounding
    as I labored pulling out bricks,
    resetting them firmly in line
    clearly establishing the boundary
    round Mother's grave.

I worked outside and in
    knowing the need to accept her death.
        That was definite.

The other boundary, harder to build,
    meant choosing death of a past love.
As I set those bricks,
    his harsh words from the night before
        kept piercing my own blurred boundaries.

Taught by pain,
    livened by work,
        I turned to tending inner boundaries.

In the Truck

We were together in the truck
    as in separate containers,
        they in front,
        I in back.

Their presence, deathlike to me.
    Impossible to let my heart speak.

I search.
    Through muddied glass
        I find flower petals
        and feel caressed
            by weavings of field lavenders and blues.

Thoughts at Dawn

At dawn, we followed the dirt path
    up through the firs.
He was walking freely.

I was searching.
    "Can you let the load within you go?"
    "Not yet," the black stone within me said.
I was thinking of yesterday.

Then he shows me the sun's coverlet
    on our hill.

Walking down, the word "forgiveness" comes.
    I think of the words "for giving."
        By forgiving we can release those we love
        and be free for giving.

Tears

He was wilting,
    needed replenishing.
I tried to give and fell.
Friends came,
    gave him water tenderly.
Watching, my tears overflowed.

Tears showed the truth;
    no doubt of my deep caring.
    Slower giving did not mean less loving;
      only that I could not.

Those tears were waters for my soul.

Rootings

That is where my truth lies,
    down in my pelvis,
    my loving center
    where it all begins,
    the place of my pain,
    emptiness and fullness.

It is a grace to love from here,
    to reach deep down inside
    like peasants' arms
    reaching into wheat bins
    bringing up the "daily bread"
    for him and me.

I reach for the grain
    and sow it alone.
It is blessed
    when he receives.

Cool Peace

Yes, I see them everywhere—
    an opened "Copa de Oro"—cup of gold,
    one star by the bell tower,
    his smile as he says, "I love you."
Clear light, cool peace flowed
    as we walked to the central square.

Times of harmony,
    like we felt last night.
"Armonía," round the table
    in that upstairs room,
        a feeling of loving and being loved.

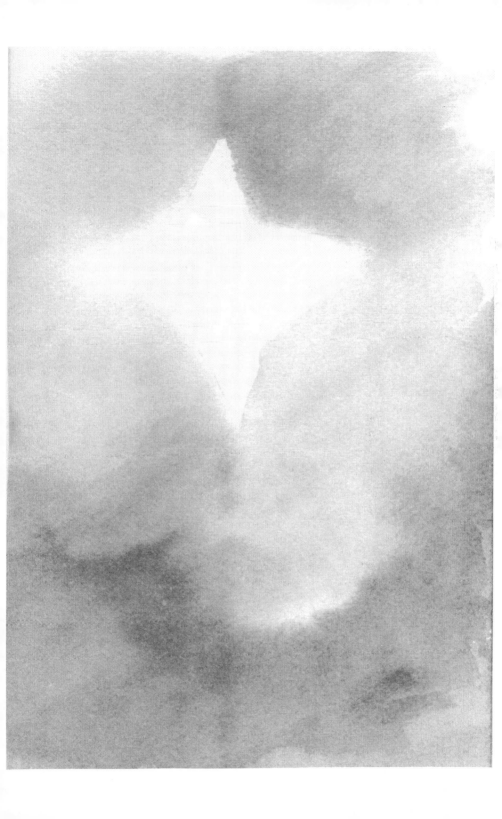

in the garden

his smile
    soothes me
words tumble
    into my ears
    like cool waters
i question
he listens and gives

leaves flourish abundant
petals blossom red

radiance

bathed in warm milk
    my body radiant

sending it forth
    to you you and you
watch be ready to receive

it is really there
    but passes invisibly
        except for some who see

Clearing

Help me to clear.
    Hold me in your wings
        that I may trust.

In darkness, surrender.
    My own way tortured.

Better, a listening prayer.

Green Lands

Let's go to those green lands
    the place of hearing healing.

Listen, listen.
    There it is.
        You are forgiven, my daughter.
        Yes, you are forgiven.
    I can forgive you.
        Will you, will you forgive?
            Of course, of course you are forgiven.

I was afraid before
    moving faster, trying harder.
Now, I want to just be in those green lands
    the place where God's love renews.

Home

Be my nest
 a place with feathers lined,
  with branches made
   cradle of my strength.

I want to be there
 surrounded by new lives,
  covered by your wings.

Then, I shall be quiet,
 trusting my new home.

Beckoning the HOLY SPIRIT

here it's dark
    i'm afraid

come come come

     pray

         wait

             watch

shhhhh

    a wisp

        a whisper

Where Is the Real Temple?

Is only Jesus' body the temple,
    his heart the altar?
What about the dark woman,
    the ugly one just killed.
        Is God in her too?

Are only Jesus' ribs the temple?
What about the murdered Salvadoran woman?
    Is it "good" to speak out for her?
        taboo—shhh—
    Pray and pray
        then speak secretly of her.

Soldiers cut her, gutted her,
    threw her to dogs.
Is she holy?

How can we find God?
Only through ritual, preaching, creeds?

Where is the real temple?

Camouflaged

Late one afternoon this November,
    I walked outside Tenancingo*
        toward the children's school.
    The road was quiet.
    Banana and coffee trees
        covered the cliff on my left.

First, I saw one, then another and another
    standing like the trees,
        leaved limbs in their boots, belts and collars.
One right beside me—I could have touched him.
    His left foot planted in the ditch
        and his right on the incline.
    He held the black barreled gun close,
        hid it with his body.
    I looked at his boyish face darkened with smudge
        and wondered who gave him orders.
        "Things are better," they say.

Death squads are careful.
    Torturers leave no mark.
    They come at night dressed in civvies,
        driving a Cherokee with dark windows.
    They stop the minister,
        yank him from his car,
        leave his child
            and three parishioners in the dark.
Black plastic over his head,
    they beat him one, two, three, four, five, days
    interrogation, no sleep.
His family cannot find him.
    What's his crime?
    He directs relief to the hungry.

"Those poor help the guerillas," they say.
    Only the Communists do that.
    Are there Communists in the plastic huts
        we saw in San Salvador?

    The earth quakes.
        Walls break.
    Hungry mothers and children
        show through the camouflage.

*Tenancingo, El Salvador—1985

Cauldron

As I walk
    along the Japanese stepping stones
        tending flowers,
            I feel that dark stone inside.

Thoughts of alchemy come:
    "don't fear,
        it's part of inner transformation."

I remember Christ's disciples
    together with their fears
        in that upstairs room
            where Christ came to them.

My body, like that upper room,
    at times, becomes a cauldron,
        a place where stones change.

Losing One's Self

I wonder—
> "Am I selfish
>> when I tighten
>> expected to do more than my share?"

It is hard to distinguish goodness and selfishness.
> Self-affirmation
>> often seems what God is asking.
> How, then, can finding one's self be losing it?

I asked—
> "Does 'losing myself'
> mean for me to wash all the dishes?"

Sometimes, with grace, we can let go
> making room to receive.

That night, inside the pool's moon,
> we probed, then found a way to lose ourselves.
> It's what's happening now,
> the search, the joy, the love between us,
> like being washed together in the moon's water.

Gift

In the noonday service,
>though trying to listen,
>>his words seem irrelevant.

Then, I hear:
>"The gifts of God for the people ... "
>>that is the smoothing beauty.
>and, as he gives me the bread,
>>he says, "bread of heaven."

Child in the Swing

I become her,
      jump on the swing,
         give a push,
            and go up to the sky.

The stars in the black dome above,
      back and forth with me.
The lights of the town mix.

The magic is real.

Slide Down from the Stars!

I climb to touch the stars
    above the cottonwoods.
Then flash down glistening silver,
    hit the earth,
    his words reverberating inside.

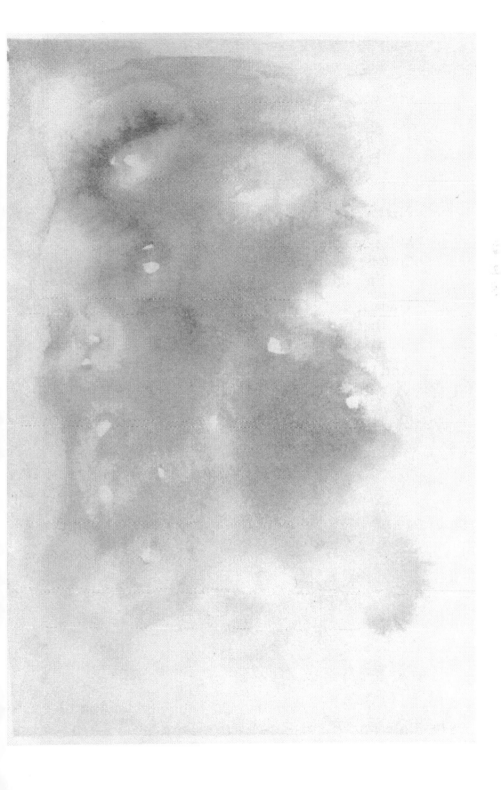

Bursting Milk Pods

Milk pods burst!
    Cottons go straight to the stars.

There it is
    that path
        swinging up and over
            from one horizon to the next.

And I can feel them
    sprinkling my head
        as I dance back from Compline.

*With affection and gratitude to
Betty Sue Flowers, Irma Grizá, June Keener Wink,
Judith Liro, Rana Pierucci and Mary Teague*

Gretchen Lara-Shartle

I was a busy child, forever asking questions and befriending strangers. My home was in a nest of pines near Houston. I remember feeling strong as I pulled screw worms out of my colt's head wound, savvy, knowing just where the armadillo's hole was in the second pasture, and wary, watching out for poisonous snakes that curled up in hens' nesting barrels. Sunday school was frustrating. No real questions were answered. So, at ten, I decided to learn on my own and buried the downy yellow ball of a chick who died in our incubator. Three days later, I found it still in its grave. It had not risen.

My cousins, a few friends, and I started the Gray Cat Club. Our main jobs were looking for buried treasures, building forts to hide from the Germans, and finding Smokey's newest litter of kittens. I always wanted to see her give birth.

In high school, our mothers took my cousins, my sister, and me to Trinidad. There, I made friends with Josephine, who supported her children on sixty-five dollars a year. I felt strangely responsible for that kind of poverty.

For college I chose Wellesley, because it was excellent and hard. There, I wanted to learn THE TRUTH. After Wellesley—India. Ancient Hindu truths salved neither the frustration I felt nor the suffering of those hands reaching for me in need.

Later, Buddhist meditation gave me permission to be quiet. This quiet land that I had begun to tend inside and out became the grounds for prayer at The Monastery of Christ in the Desert. At times, my faith, a gossamer thread, seems real. This fragile thread, like a spider's web, now connects me to God and others and is close to my source of inspiration.

As On Earth and In Heaven, was beginning to take shape I asked Irma Griza, whom I love as a sister-friend and admire as an outstanding Mexican artist to paint her visions of my poems. During the month we spent together in San Anselmo, California, I wrote a new poem every day.

Now together, we offer these poems and paintings to you.

Irma Grizá

I am because I paint.
My painting is a reflection of me, of
what I search for and care about.
It lets me say who I am.
Thus, I disclose my emotions, my
consciousness of life, my daily struggles.
Every conflict within me bursts onto the
canvas and there becomes clear.
For me, being a good artist comes first.
I must paint well before I can express myself.
I am because I paint, and because I paint, I am.

Irma Grizá was born in Mexico City. She studied painting at the National School of Plastic Arts (Academia de San Carlos) of the National Autonomous University of Mexico. Since then, she has dedicated her life to painting.

With sixty-four years of professional life as an artist, her extensive work has been exhibited in around forty individual exhibitions and dozens of group shows, in galleries and museums in Mexico, the United States, and France.

In March 2017, she presented the exhibition Epifanía del Silencio at the Gallery of the Autonomous Metropolitan University (UAM), Cuajimalpa campus, in Mexico City.

Her previous solo exhibition, Constellations of the Impossible, a traveling exhibition (2016—17), which began at the "Carlos Olvera" Museum of Modern Art in Toluca, was later presented at the Manuel Felguérez Museum of Abstract Art in Zacactecas, and finally at the Museum of Mexico City.

Collectively, she participated in the exhibition Mexican Masks, Veiled Symbolism at the National Palace (2015—16).

She took part in the project The Artists Responsible in the Defense of Fauna, a book and collection of ostrich eggs by sixty artists, presented in December 2014 at the Rufino Tamayo Contemporary Art Museum in Mexico City.

In 2012, the book Fatigas del Drawing, by Irma Grizá and Luis Ignacio Sáinz, was jointly published by the UAM Azcapotzalco and Aguijón del Astro.

Her solo exhibition The Manifestations of

Absence ran from October 2008 to April 2010 in three important Mexican museums: the Anthropology Museum of Xalapa, the Museum of the Cultures of Oaxaca (a former convent), and the Regional Museum of Guadalajara.

Her individual exhibition Suspended Realities had great success at the Museum of Modern Art of the Mexiquense Institute of Culture in Toluca (2006) and at Presences, in the Metropolitan Gallery of the UAM, in Mexico City (2005).

In 1990 Irmá obtained one of the Paris Awards granted by the Group of Sixteen, Asociación Civil, to exhibit in the French capital.

In 1975, she was awarded first place in a competition of the Salón de la Plástica Mexicana, the official gallery of the National Institute of Fine Arts in Mexico City. She has had group and individual shows at the Salón in 1976, '77, '79, '80, and '83. She has also had individual shows of her paintings at Club de Banqueros de México in 1983; Dickinson College in Carlisle, Pennsylvania, in 1965; and The Little Gallery in Philadelphia, in 1962.

Art critics and writers such as: Raquel Tibol, Luis Ignacio Sáinz, Alberto Ruy Sánchez, Hugo Hiriart, José María Espinasa, Eliseo Alberto, Francisco Serrano, Alfonso Alfaro, and Margarita de Orellana, among others, have written about her work.

Irmá still lives in Mexico City.